THINGS THAT MAKE YOU LOVE AND HATE FEAR

TRUTH THAT CAN'T BE IGNORE

BOSCO EKKA

ISBN 979-888555680-4

Contents

Preface

Fear is an inherent element of being human. People get terrified when they have a bad dream. People are fearful of change. People are afraid of fresh opportunities. Fear, on the other hand, has been portrayed as negative. As a society, we have come to believe that fear is a negative emotion that should be avoided at all costs. That's not the case at all, and you should know it. When it comes to adolescence, fear plays a significant influence.

Because they're terrified, some individuals conceal their heads to evade the situation at hand. Do it anyhow, even when you're afraid. Other individuals are motivated by fear and take action. Three distinct groups of individuals are unable to move for fear of being discovered. It's possible to put your anxieties on the back burner and live your life the way you want to.

JOY is the exact opposite of FEAR in terms of opposites. Anything that isn't based on love has to do with fear, in my opinion. Your thoughts and emotions conflict when you're terrified. Some people may react with anger because they fear losing their feeling of control. Sadness may be the source of all evil.

How Come Death Is So Scary? Humans are terrified of the dark in the same way that a child is. - A slice of smoked meat. Many individuals are terrified of death for many reasons, but the most prevalent one is because they are afraid of the unknown.

When it comes to manifesting your desires, do you realise the debilitating effects of fear? Fear is what separates a millionaire from the average Joe. This is a simple task that doesn't need any training or skill. Do you have any questions concerning fear?

Everyone has a fear that manifests itself at some time in their lives. Everyone's afraid of the dark when they're young, especially of monsters under their beds. We or someone else may have created this fear.

My fear of failing was the greatest obstacle to realising the vision I had for my organisation. Dread, lack of confidence, or any other unknown fear prevented me from realising my full potential and achieving my objectives. According to Franklin D. Roosevelt, "the only thing to fear in building your firm is your dread itself."

Fear can terrify people. I'm assuming that's the goal, but how often and how intensely should we be alarmed? It's possible to experience two different kinds of terror at the same time. Only true fear has the power to rescue you.

An alternative to Medication for the Treatment of Phobias is possible. A person with agoraphobia, claustrophobia or panic attacks may have phobias such as flying, heights and insects or even going to school (fear of going outside, of being away from the security of the home, or of being alone).

When it comes to marketing, have you ever been paralysed by the fear of rejection? Fear of failure or fear of making a mistake when it comes to reaching out to others? It's something that many of us have by default, in my opinion. With this, it is we can't get enough of this. Learn exactly how I overcome some of my worries and stepped out in a big win this article.

The most common reason people avoid the dentist is fear, Prickly feelings. Some individuals get anxious during drills. Is there anything you can do to alleviate that stress? Gaining new patients by making them feel comfortable is an excellent approach to increase recommendations for your practice.

Fear of achievement is often the culmination of previous phobias. The anxiety may stem from putting their faith in you. Because success may represent so many different things to so many different individuals, it is impossible to generalise a universal dread of success.

What terrifies us? Are you terrified of something? We're stumped as to what to do. We've all felt fear to varying degrees throughout our lives. I conducted my research and found that the most plant anxieties were public speaking and fear of success.

Our apprehensions of being rejected, failing, or succeeding in business—not to mention shame and criticism—keep us from moving forward.

The children are left alone for most of the day because they attend school. Parents used to worry that their kids would miss after school nonattendance money for lunch, but those days are long gone. Using mobile phones might potentially provide a new set of risks.

CHAPTER ONE

I am terrified of meeting new people

When you're human, fear is a part of who you are. A dream makes people afraid. Change makes people afraid. There is a lot of fear that comes with new chances. Yet, fear has been made to look bad. We have come to think that fear is bad and something to avoid or get rid of. That's not true at all. Fear plays a big and important role in how we grow up and how we grow up.

Laura Berman Fortgang, who wrote "Take Yourself to the Top," said that "every choice you make is based either on fear or on courage." Fear and courage are like the two sides of the same coin. In the air, which side have you been getting when you throw the coin? If you're afraid all the time, try these tips to make fear your friend. Until then, your coin won't be able to land on courage.

To deal with your fear rather than react to it: Listen to your fear as you would a trusted friend. Take your fear to the end. When you're afraid, don't act on it.

Is there a natural way you deal with fear in your life? Many times, we just act. Retaliate. We stop, change direction, settle for something less scary, or ignore it and keep going even though we're afraid. None of them is the best way to use our fears. These reactions, on the other hand, stop us from fully achieving what we want or dream of.

Making friends with fear is the first step. You have to stop reacting to your fear and start responding to it instead. Our fears are there because they want us to know something about ourselves. Then we make changes, fix something, or make something that we need. At the first sign of fear, pause, listen, and respond, and then do it again. The longer you don't pay attention to it, the more likely you are to act on it and regret it.

It's like you would listen to a friend. Suppose you saw your fears as friends instead. What would your friend want to tell you? What is it telling you to do? When we're afraid, we usually try to get rid of the "bad" feelings that come with it. There are things about it that make us uncomfortable, and we want to get away from them.

It's time to enjoy it! as if it were a friend. It's not asking you to give up on your hopes and dreams, your opportunities, or your chances. You are being asked for a lot more from this than you should be. It wants you to act bigger. When you want to be self-interested and protect yourself. Dream big, but be careful. Have a Plan B ready. Plan C, too. Build a safety net so that you can get back up and keep going instead of having to spend time and energy putting things together. If you don't want to be rejected, accept yourself fully.

In case you're afraid of something, try this: Write down the messages that make you feel afraid. If I don't do well, what will happen? Suppose this doesn't work. Then what? Then what? I am afraid that I will lose. What message is my friend's fear trying to convey to me? What is it telling me to do? Is this true? For each message that is based on the fear that you have written down, write down your answer.

Finally, think about this question: what would I be like if these messages hadn't come to me?

Take your fear to the very end. Recently, I talked about fear with a young entrepreneur. Because he didn't want to do well at something, he said that was his biggest fear. I didn't know what failure was. He said that he had lost all of his family's money, savings, and home and was broke. In that case, what would happen? What would you do next? Then I asked. His answer: "I'd start over." I would also never let it get that far. I would leave before I lost my house and all of my money. "OK, then, what do you need to do to make sure you and your family don't lose everything?" After a few minutes of writing down what had to be done, his fear was gone. A lot of people had heard of it and responded to it. It had been taken to its natural conclusion, too. A lot of things are now clear. His coin could now flip to courage because he knew for sure that he would be fine if his business failed. This was not the only way he could fail. He could try something else. Instead, it was keeping his family going that was the most important thing for him to do. Then, he needs something else from him... something he knows how to make happen.

It's easy to get along with your fears. In the dark, look at your fears. Ask them what they want you to know, and what you should do. If something happens, keep asking, "What if that happens?" and soon you will know the answer to that question, as well. You will figure out what to do. You will have responded to the fear rather than reacted to it, and you will have done this instead. You'll make a new friend who is afraid. With your friend fear right behind you, flip that coin and start acting out of courage.

CHAPTER TWO

Face your fears and push through.

Some people hide their heads to avoid what's in front of them because they're afraid. Feel the fear and do it anyway. Fear is a motivator for other people, and it makes them want to act. There are three groups of people who can't move at all because they are afraid. Putting your fears on the shelf and living your way can be done.

Do I agree that this isn't a new title? It's taken from one of my favourite books by Susan Jeffers, who wrote the book with the same title. It's interesting to see how people react to fear. Fear makes some people hide their heads and play ostriches so they can't see what's in front of them. Fear is a motivator for other people, and it makes them want to act. There are three groups of people who can't move at all because they are afraid.

One of the most common issues I hear from my clients is that they can't live the life they truly want. This means that they can't make money, connect with others, or feed their souls. The most common answer I get when I ask them what's stopping them from making that happen for themselves: "I'm afraid I won't be able to because I have a mortgage." "What will my wife/husband/family think about this?" "After I retire, I'll be able to do that," I said. It sounds like a lot of these things. Around 10 years ago or so, when I was thinking about changing jobs, I came across a company called Changing Course, which was run by Valerie Young. Valerie has a website where she talks about how her mother died of a heart attack at the age of 61, five months before Valerie was supposed to retire and before she could do all the things she had planned to do when she retired. Valerie tells her storey on her website. Bam! This storey hit me right in the face. I was shocked by it. It had been a long time since I had been happy with my job. I wondered every day, "Will I ever be happy again?" "Is this it? Is this the life I was so excited about after college?" A mid-life crisis had already begun for me at the time. I was only about 32 years old at the time. How could I be so young? People are supposed to wait until they are at least 40 before going through this. A lot of people were starting to think of me as crazy.

I remember having a lot of conversations with my now-ex-husband about this issue and what each of us wanted from life. It became clear that he was happy to settle for whatever life gave him. This isn't true for me. I'm very driven, and I wanted to see how far I could go by taking the bull by the horns and seeing how far I could go. As the parade went by, I thought of him sitting on his porch while I was out in the parade. It was also not in my best interest to wait until our retirement to start living the way I wanted to, as he suggested. Valerie's mom, for example, might not live long enough for that to happen, so I didn't want to wait. It was like talking to a brick wall because he didn't understand what we were talking about.

Ten years later, I'm not where I want to be, but I'm much closer than I would have been if I'd kept going the way I was at 32. I changed. I decided that I was going to stop being afraid. No, I didn't care about what anyone else thought. I've always been a risk-taker in my family. I've done things that none of them had ever done or even thought about. However, I've never thought of the risks as "fly-by-the-seat-of-your-pants" risks. Instead, I've thought of them as strategic risks. At some points, it might have been only me who saw the plan.

That's right. I wanted to be closer to my family, so I convinced my ex that we wanted to move to Texas, took a virtual assistant training programme, and finished it. I quit my job and took a temp job until I could get the business going and until we moved. I found out that my ex didn't want to move, so I filed for divorce, put the house on the market, and found a place to live with my mom in the bedroom in her house. Then, people make fun of me when I won't go on a roller coaster. I think that's easy when you're going through a big change in your life. No, I don't think any of you should face your fears in this way. At least not without a parachute and a lot of padding, though. Everybody has fears, but if you run or own a business, those fears are even bigger. "How will I pay this month's bills?" What if that person doesn't want to hire me? Do not want to make sales calls: Does this person need my money? The thing you're afraid of is probably what stands in your way of getting what you want. Don't let fear rule your life. Use your fear as a motivator to get to the next level in your life, business, or job.

Think about how frightening it can be to have the fear stay with you all the time. It has a way of sneaking up on you when you least expect it. I can hear it rustling in the background right now because I'm thinking about a new way to grow my business.

CHAPTER THREE

Getting Rid of the Pain

Fear's polar opposite is joy. I believe that fear is at the root of anything that isn't loving. When you're afraid, your mind and your emotions are at odds. Anger, for example, maybe a response to a fear of losing one's sense of control. Sadness may be the root of all evil.

Fear's polar opposite is joy. I believe that fear is at the root of anything that isn't loving. When you're afraid, your mind and your emotions are at odds. Anger, for example, maybe a response to a fear of losing one's sense of control. Fear of what you've lost or may lose is a common cause of sadness. "How do you let go and walk away from fear?" is, of course, the million-dollar question. Jim Britt, a founding member of Quanta, explains.

There is a common desire among individuals to do more in their lives. Facing their fears, they decide not to even attempt it. Because of the friction, it causes in your thinking, fear paralyses you. An entrepreneur's dream of starting their firm is a fantastic example to consider. Those who are afraid of the unknown, of danger, or of failure may never get started. A fearful state of mind is a natural response from your brain, which is only attempting to keep you safe. You may fear taking a risk by trying something you've never done before. As soon as you feel pain, your brain will tell you to leave.

Getting rid of fear may be accomplished via a variety of methods. Fear, after all, is not a myth; it is, in fact, extremely real. The narrative is a fabrication, but one that you believe to be real. And it will come to pass for you if you have faith in it.

Face your fears and they will go away, "is a common cure-all." Do you have any concerns regarding those who are afraid of "confronting their fears?" There are a slew of commonplace activities that, if seen as hazardous, might arouse anxiety. Taking the wheel of an automobile carries a degree of danger. Getting married is a big decision that comes with a lot of uncertainty. A bicycle ride is a perilous endeavour. Skiing in the snow is a high-risk activity. Climbing mountains is a dangerous sport. Taking up the responsibility of raising a family is a risk. It's dangerous to drive faster than the posted limit. And so on and so on and so foand so onso forth. Despite the dangers, we continue to engage in these activities. As you can see, everything you do is either motivated by fear or by love.

If you're moving toward your goals, you're also moving away from your worries. The more you work toward your goals, the more you'll be able to let go of your fears. You may still experience dread while you make progress toward your passions. It's important, though, to pay attention to your fears and see them for what they are. The energy you associate with dread is derived from a recurrence of a negative event in the past, which you then extrapolate into the future.

In order to understTone must first understand what it is. "FEAR is just taking a previous event, projecting it into the future, and reliving it in the present moment." Jim Britt's statement. You can only give fear life if you allow it to exist in the first place. If you're moving toward your goals, you're also moving away from your worries. The more you work toward your goals, the more you'll be able to let go of your fears. You will experience terror as you come closer to what you really want. It's important, though, to pay attention to your fears and see them for what they are. The energy you associate with dread is derived from a recurrence of a negative event in the past, which you then extrapolate into the future. is nothing more than a manifestation of a person's inability to let go of the energy that has been

As soon as you recognise your fear for what it actually is, you will decrease its grip on you. Alternatively, I'd like to refer to it as your grip on it. In the process of self-reflection, you're letting go of your fears. This is a level above self-awareness. Being conscious of fear is one thing, but removing oneself from it and recognising it for what it is is another.

Fear is nothing more than a figment of your imagination based on a re-enactment of something that has already happened in the past. You are letting go of your fear when you self-observe it and perceive it for what it is. After that, all you have to do is go on to what you really like.

CHAPTER FOUR

The Ability To Develop A Positive Relationship With Death

Why Are We Afraid of Dying? Humans have the same dread of the dark as a little kid. - A rasher of bacon There are many reasons why people are afraid of death, but the most common explanation is because we are afraid of the unknown.

Why Do We Dread Death?

"Men are afraid of death as though they were afraid of the dark." Bacon is an excellent source of protein.

We dread death for a variety of reasons, but perhaps the most compelling is that it is unknown to the vast majority of people. We are afraid of what will happen to us when we die because we don't know what will happen to us when we die. Some individuals are terrified of dying because they believe it will be excruciatingly painful. In the end, there is no suffering. Even for people with severe illnesses like cancer, dying may be a serene and quiet experience.

Pain from surface wounds such as bed sores or deep pain such as bone or nerve discomfort may be so unbearable that death may even be welcomed by the patient of a terminal disease. It's important to recognise the difference between physical agony and the process of death. The degradation of the physical body is not a part of the dying process, which is unique. There is no agony when you die.

When a person dies, all of their body's physiological processes come to an end, including their ability to breathe. When this happens, the heart stops beating and the blood stops flowing. As the body's ability to produce heat diminishes, so does the body's temperature. The death process entails much more than simply physical death to people who think we are spiritual beings rather than just physical creatures.

To enter the spiritual world, we must let go of our physical bodies via death. Because our apprehension about mortality stems from our lack of familiarity with it, it makes sense to educate ourselves about it. It's less frightening when we comprehend death. Death, like our friends, should be cultivated as a friendship and we should know it as we know our loved ones.

Three easy approaches may help us develop a close relationship with death: The first step is to connect with God. Instead of placing blame, develop the practice of accepting responsibility. Bless others around you. Set up a line of communication with God. When we build a connection with God, we connect with our spirituality. God can be whatever you want him to be. This might imply an all-powerful deity for believers in Christianity, Islam, or Hinduism. In Buddhism, it may refer to one's own Buddha seed. Atheists can face up to their spirituality.

Having a spiritual connection with God entails regaining your faith. It helps you connect with your spiritual self. There is so much more to us than our bodily self. Only our spiritually lives on when we die, leaving our physical bodies behind. Because of this, we need to be acquainted with our spirituality to better understand ourselves. When we die, it is the only part of us that will live on. This "truth," as it's often known, is accepted by almost every major religion.

Develop the Habit of Forgiveness.

When wonderful things happen to us, we take them as a sign that we deserve them or have worked hard for them, but when bad things happen to us, we search for someone or something else to blame immediately. This is particularly true when we are faced with tragedies like terminal diseases. After blaming God, we may shift the responsibility to ourselves or others.

Whether good or terrible things happen to us, we should strive to maintain a state of neutrality. When bad things happen, it's easy to feel depressed and cynical about life. We prolong our agony by looking for someone or something to blame. When we fight death, it becomes a foe, but when we embrace it, it becomes a comrade.

A habit of acceptance does not imply that we do nothing to change our circumstances. However, building a practice of acceptance does not mean that we do nothing. It does not imply, for example, that we do nothing when we are told we have a fatal disease. Only if therapy is readily accessible should we consider it. On the other hand, it implies that we must be aware of and prepared to accept the fact that no more curative therapy options exist.

Only when we refuse to confront death do we feel terror. Sadly, many would take advantage of our dread of mortality to market their 'treatment'. It is very uncommon for the terminally sick to be deceived into giving up their wealth and property in the hope of finding a cure.

Allow Yourself to be Used by God in the Service of Others.

When it comes to death, this is our strongest and most dependable friend. Death becomes less frightening when we know that we've done good deeds for others and that we've strived to live a blameless life. If we've lived a good life, with no bad intentions toward other living things, we have nothing to be afraid of when it's time to go. As a result, our minds will be at rest. When they cross the bridge to the other side, individuals who live selfish lives and injure others to gain personal gain will be imprisoned in small, gloomy cells.

To make the most of our time, we should do our best for the planet and those around us. Help others by removing some of their burdens. Bring happiness to those who are sad and solace to those who are suffering. There are a lot of people in this world who are worse off than we are. To be a benefit to others, we must first count our blessings.

CHAPTER FIVE

When it comes to the Law of Attraction, fear is the only thing keeping you from achieving your goals.

Do you realise exactly how damaging fear is to your capacity to attract what you desire? It's fear that makes the difference between a billionaire and a poor person. No education or talent is required for this. Is there anything you'd want to know about fear?

The best secret to overcoming anything you could possibly conceive would you trust me if I told you about it? Would you be sceptical if I told you that you could materialise a million dollars in the next thirty days using the Law of Attraction?

The best part about this little-known fact is that even if you know what it is, you'll have a terrible time cracking it without the right equipment. In order to properly use the law of attraction, you must first become conscious of the anxieties you have about attracting what you want.

Just consider the subject of money. Have you ever observed how many sophisticated spiritual leaders with extraordinary powers of manifestation are also struggling to make ends meet?

That someone who understands how to use the power of the law of attraction and materialise yet is still poor is a bit of a mystery. You're not able to get what you really want because of your anxieties that 1) you're not deserving of it. 2) You're afraid you're not up to the task. As a result, you worry that you won't be able to get your hands on it. As a result, you're apprehensive about the duty that comes with it. There is a sense of dread that comes with possessing it.

Because your worries become your beliefs, you may not have been able to materialise the things you wanted because you didn't realise this. There are two kinds of people in this world: those who are afraid and those who are confident. The difference between the two is that those who are afraid and those who are confident are able to overcome their fear through the power of their vision.

Raising your energy to such high levels that it acts as a vortex to draw in the things you want to create might transform lesser emotions like fear and uncertainty. When it comes to manifesting, understanding of the law of attraction alone isn't enough. To materialise, you must learn how to modify your own state of being at a much more finger-level level.

If you can raise the intensity of your fears to a greater level, abundance will be yours. You may more readily attract a prosperous existence. You may easily alter the world by submitting articles.

CHAPTER SIX

Do You Constantly Panic?

There's something everyone is afraid of at some point in their life. We're all terrified of the dark and of monsters lurking in our beds as kids. This is a fabricated dread, either by ourselves or by someone else.

Fear is a natural human response to new experiences and situations. Fear of the dark and monsters lurking beneath our beds are common childhood phobias. This is a dread that has been instilled in us by someone or something external, such as a movie or television show. Is this something that should be avoided by a child? Even if parents don't tell their children that there are no monsters lurking about the house, their children will eventually grow out of this fear.

Fear of heights, water, aircraft, and a host of other potential life experiences is often the result of prior trauma or uninformed preconceptions. Education and training may often reduce a person's anxiety about participating in a certain activity or travelling by car or aircraft. On the other hand, fear is a beneficial thing because it prevents people from doing things that might put them in harm's way without proper training or instruction. It's impossible to get rid of all your anxieties since they're a part of your DNA. There are certain anxieties that can never be conquered, such as a fear of heights, and they should be acknowledged. Somewhere in each and every one of us lurks a phobia that we will never be able to get over.

The dread of losing one's job, failing a task, or failing an exam is genuine, but it does not put one's life at risk. Preparation and training are usually all that is needed to overcome difficulties. It's OK to be fearful of things we don't know how to do, but it's also important to recognise that we need more practise in order to succeed. In this situation, the dread serves as a signal to seek further information or training.

Dread of harming yourself or your loved ones is the worst fear. The dread of being shot, raped, robbed, or otherwise physically abused is a genuine one, and we must arm ourselves with knowledge in order to guard against it. Everyone must first and foremost avoid putting oneself in harm's path. As a general rule, it's a poor idea to go about in the dark or approach dangerous areas on your own. We can avoid much of the risk if we avoid these regions. Desperate individuals may, however, rob, rape, and beat up nice people in well-lit parking lots and structures.

Your house should be a place where you feel comfortable and secure, a place where you can relax and recharge your batteries. Unfortunately, there are terrible individuals out there who will break into your home in order to steal your belongings or, worse, cause you damage. Is there anything you can do to ensure that you aren't forced to spend your life in constant anxiety?

If you must visit a location where you fear you may be in danger, go with a buddy who is competent or go in a group. As previously said, you should not put yourself in harmful situations. Carry a stun gun, MACE, or pepper spray in public to keep yourself safe from attackers. These things will temporarily take your attacker's weaponry away from him, allowing you to flee and call the police for help.

There are numerous things you can do both inside and outside your house to make it a safer place to live. External lights should be operating properly and illumination should be provided at all entrances as well as possible hazard areas. For the most part, motion-activated lights are less costly to acquire and run than traditional lighting systems. Motion-activated lights may be placed on your building's corners and in trouble spots. Trim your shrubs to prevent them from acting as a hiding place for criminals. Having a light above the garage door can make it easier to get out of your vehicle when it's dark outside.

There are vulnerable points within your house that might be exploited by intruders. Get a door bar for sliding patio doors to keep them from slamming shut. It is recommended that all outside doors have a deadbolt lock that requires a key to operate on both sides. The first level of your home should be protected against intruders by installing sturdier windows or barricades. It is simple and affordable to set up a wireless burglar alarm, window alarm, or door alarm. The sound of a dog barking might dissuade burglars from breaking into your house while you're away. The cops may be called automatically if a comprehensive system is set up.

A time-stamped video of a burglary in progress is indisputable evidence in a courtroom. For less than $600, you can have a four-camera setup. Recording and internet connectivity let you to monitor your house at any time from a computer or mobile device. It is possible to hide a single hidden camera or nanny camera in your house, and it will seem to be an everyday item. A babysitter or your children might be recorded by these devices. Anywhere you go, you can plug in a DVR-equipped hidden camera and start recording. Removing the video card gives you access to your video, which you can then watch on your computer.

You don't have to be afraid! You may feel more secure if you have the proper training and self-defense gear. Insurance premiums may be reduced by installing security cameras, security lighting, and deadbolt locks.

CHAPTER SEVEN

How to Begin a New Company?

When it came to turning my company's vision into a reality, I was most challenged by my fear of failure. When I was unable to realise my full potential because of a lack of confidence, fear, or any other unknown fear, I was unable to accomplish my goals. To paraphrase FDR, "the only thing to fear in establishing your company is your fear itself," is what I've learnt from personal experience.

There is no reason why your concept, service, or product cannot be a success with adequate study, preparation, and allocation of responsibilities. As you work toward achieving your objectives, you must keep an eye on the here and now, but you should also keep your eye on the future. Use unconventional tools, techniques, and procedures that are required to thrive in business to keep things fresh. Today, we have unprecedented access to all of the materials and tools we could need to educate ourselves on a wide range of business-related topics of interest.

The real issue is, how can I get the most out of the enormous array of options at my disposal? How do you get started in business? Visit a consulting company that provides step-by-step instructions. We provide services ranging from basic incorporation consultation packages to more sophisticated, comprehensive, and complete company packages that include marketing, public relations, advertising, and financial services for a very reasonable fee. The Motivated Entrepreneur is an all-inclusive consulting agency.

There are a wide variety of sites to get business resources and information on the Internet. As was indicated above, The Motivated Entrepreneur is a fantastic internet resource for business knowledge. However, SBA.gov, the website of the Small Business Administration, is the best place to go for verified information. It doesn't matter whether you want to work with a business consultant or do it all on your own, you should always check the official website of the government for information on how to proceed.

Start arranging your knowledge and material so that you can establish an overall strategy and begin to incorporate this strategy into your company plan & organisational structure. Before you can put your ideas on paper, you must first draft a preliminary business plan that will serve as the basis for your final company plan. This will give you a fresh set of eyes to evaluate your ideas, and it's a valuable tool for determining the legal structure that'll work best for your company's structure from a tax standpoint.

As you approach it, you should divide your preliminary business strategy into pieces. Here's a quick method to getting your ideas down on paper.

Introduction

- Describe the firm and its objectives in great detail. To get a job, it is important to list your talents and experience.

- Talk about the benefits you and your company have over your rivals.

Marketing

- Describe the items and services you provide and determine whether or not there is a market for them.
- Determine the size and geography of your target market.

Accounting and budgeting

- For the first year, create a monthly operational budget. For the first year, calculate the estimated return on investment and monthly cash flow.

Operations

- Describe the day-to-day operations of the company.
- Talk about recruiting and staff policies.
- Keep track of the tools you'll need to make your goods and services.
- Ensure that goods and services are produced and delivered on time.

The Ending Observation

- Express your dedication to the success of your firm by summarising your business aims and objectives.

Congratulations! You have a preliminary draft of your company plan and are considering filing for incorporation. The next phase is here... A lot of research is going on. As I indicated at the outset of this post, we have a significant advantage in today's culture because of our easy access to the vast quantity of publicly available data. Start thinking about your legal structure and what kind of organisation is ideal for you and your business, not just right now but in the future as well. I've compiled a list of things to keep in mind when you begin the process of incorporation. You may also hire a complete service consulting business that provides guidance from a variety of angles, including legal and tax issues, as well as the management of growth.

One of the most critical considerations to be made when starting a new company is the organization's structure. Consider the following while deciding whether or not to form a company entity:

Restrictions imposed by the law

Assumption of liabilities

The nature of the business

Distribution of profits

Amounts needed

The Sole Proprietorship is the most straightforward business structure. It's also the least priced, and there aren't as many obstacles to getting started with it. The majority of small companies begin as sole proprietorships, which means that the business's assets and earnings belong solely to the business's founder(s). It is also possible to disband the company if requested, which is a plus. As a single owner, you're legally liable for any obligations against the firm, which is a drawback. As a result, they may be unable to get traditional sources of funding and instead be forced to rely on personal resources or consumer loans.

The Partnership is another common type of incorporation. A partnership is simple to set up, but it must be governed by a written agreement. Partners in a corporation have limitless responsibility, but they also get all of the company's profits. Raising money is easier when you have more than one partner on board, but arguments might arise since decisions are made jointly.

The corporation is the last kind of legal organisation. The legal definition of a company separates it from its owners. Without an attorney, it's possible to form a company, but it's best to get legal guidance first. Corporations are often the most difficult and expensive to set up than the other two types of company structures. Ownership of shares is a prerequisite for exercising control. People having the most stock ownership, not total shareholders, are in charge of the company. Shareholders may only be held liable to a limited extent for the company's debts or judgements.

It takes more time and money to incorporate a business than to create a non-profit organisation, and companies are subject to more scrutiny by the federal, state, and certain municipal governments. A Subchapter S-corporation or a Limited Liability Corporation may be a better fit for your business's structure than a C-corporation. Consult with an expert before making a decision on the best corporate structure for your firm.

CHAPTER EIGHT

Transforming Anxiety into Excitation

People are frightened by fear. I assume that's what it's meant to do, but how frequently and how much should we feel scared? Two types of fear exist. You can only be saved by genuine dread.

People get frightened because of their own fears. I assume that's what it's meant to do, but how frequently and how much should we feel scared? Two types of dread exist apprehension and apprehension. When faced with a difficult circumstance, real terror may save your life (like being chased by a predator or facing imminent danger). Imagined anxieties, however, keep you from enjoying life to the fullest. Imagined concerns may be based on prior negative experiences, other people's anxieties, or incorrect information. In the eyes of your brain, there is no distinction between an imagined dread and a genuine one.

As you prepare for new experiences, fear may cause stress and bodily uneasiness. It may impair your ability to make sensible decisions or lead you to act irrationally. Terror and full immobility might result from a person's tendency to be fearful. As an alternative, you might transform your fear into a thrilling edge while pushing beyond your comfort zone. The things that terrify some people are a joy to others. You'll feel great about yourself and gain a lot of self-confidence when you face your anxieties.

You will be happier whether your activities are driven by fear or by bravery. Fear has little value in today's environment, particularly if the apparent anxiety is based on nothing more than irrationality. When you're paralysed by anxiety, you start to obsess about things that will never happen. We have concerns about the state of the environment, our immediate surroundings, and the state of the planet. Murderers, terrorists and the stock market all occupy our thoughts. Worrying is one thing, but being realistic is another. As a matter of fact, worrying is a waste of time; it hasn't paid any bills nor prevented any hurricanes. It's pointless to stress over something that can be fixed. If you can't do anything to fix your difficulties, there's no use in fretting.

Think about your anxieties and concerns and how they affect your degree of enjoyment in your life. Just examine whether or not your anxieties are actually looking out for your best interests. Are you focused on the negative rather than the positive? So many individuals are obsessed with concern, hoping that one day their life would improve, as another day passes. Instead of thinking about the worst-case scenario, imagine the greatest. Become an inverted paranoid, as described by motivational speaker Brian Tracey. Persuade yourself that you will always be surrounded by individuals eager to provide you with some type of pleasure or amusement. Consider the world to be out to get you.

The truth is, enjoyable people, don't pretend to be fearless. What happens when people confront their fears?

To a certain extent, yes, but those who are dedicated joy detectors make it a point to face their concerns head-on rather than cowering in dread beneath the covers. They transform their anxieties into adrenaline-fueled surges of euphoria and exhilaration. A winner is someone who has the courage to confront their fears, regardless of whether or not they are overcome. To win, all you have to do is choose to be driven by your enthusiasm for life rather than your dread of death.

Gaining information may help you overcome your fears and anxieties. When venturing out into the world, rely on your intelligence rather than your fears. Going on a mountain hike, would you be concerned that you would slip and fall or get lost or devoured by a bear? Or what about being caught up in an avalanche? These are all plausible outcomes, but they're merely speculative at best. Worrying about it increases your likelihood of conceiving of it. In order to be safe, you should steer clear of dangerous areas such as steep drops, avoid strapping fish to your body, and avoid avalanche zones.

We do so many risky things in our daily lives, but we're afraid of a little risk. Isn't it safe to cross the street? Do you think you'll ever get hit by a bus? You, of course, don't believe me. Why, therefore, do we conjure up such dreadful images when contemplating new or uncharted territory? Crossing a busy roadway is a much higher risk of serious harm than hiking in the mountains. It's better to be alive if anything happens when you're having fun. Watching TV and eating potato chips may keep you safe, but you'll gain weight and find it tedious to sit around all day doing nothing.

The person who refuses to go snorkelling because he or she is afraid of sharks or other sea creatures is the one who loses. The underwater world's enchantment is something you'll never be able to see. Although it's possible that a water monster may swoop in while you're playing, the odds are really low. Either you'll be struck by lightning or you'll win an Olympic gold medal. This has happened many times before, and it hasn't killed anybody. Because you've been picked out, what's the point?

The golden rule of adventure is to put safety first, however you may minimise the risk by adhering to this guideline. Reduce the risk as much as possible. Wearing safety gear is encouraged if it is available. If common sense is required, then apply it. Take the necessary precautions to protect yourself. Do you need a life jacket, a helmet, or any other particular equipment to participate in this sport? Isn't it possible to get knowledge from someone who has already achieved success? While it's true that a few of individuals die each year while out having a good time, most of the time it's because they haven't taken enough safety measures. So don't be naive. Being foolish and dead at the same time is not a good combination. Being both dead and ignorant at the same time is a major source of shame. AVOID AT ALL COSTS.. Let's assume you've always wanted to try your hand at kayaking. When kayaking, you'll have a better time if you can swim and self-rescue. You'll be better prepared to confront the world if you know how to reduce the hazard in any activity. Anxieties may be reduced to a minimum via education. "They're no better than me-I can do this!" becomes more confident when you encounter more individuals doing the same thing. You may be surprised to learn that the activity you thought was perilous really isn't.

As a result, you've gathered some information and made plans for a safe experience, but you're still too afraid to ride the roller coaster or dance on the dance floor. Then, instead of being scared, become ecstatic. Face your apprehensions and get through with the task at hand. Consider yourself fortunate to have a system that alerts you to danger and allows you to enhance your senses as a result. Let it thrill your toes and appreciate the surge of energy that comes with it. Excitement will be amplified by the fear you feel. The end result will be a lovely feeling of confidence, pride, and reliving your journey. You may be apprehensive now. An further benefit of being terrified is that it increases the level of enjoyment you get from a pleasant activity.

The majority of your anxieties are unfounded and should be dismissed as such. Learn to tell the difference between legitimate anxieties and those that are irrational. Challenge your fear, and the thing you're afraid of will go. Think about what you'd do if you weren't afraid, and then take action. Amazing things happen when you face your worries. Never lose sight of the fact that you are the one in charge.

Your happiness is built one brick at a time when you face your worries head-on. The strength you receive from overcoming one little fear will help you overcome all of your other fears. Go to an expert for assistance if you can't manage your anxieties or if you have a panic condition. Your self-esteem, confidence, and pleasure will skyrocket after you conquer your irrational concerns. To help you on your way, arm yourself with both bravery and knowledge. Make a strategy to overcome your worries if you want to do an enjoyable activity but are hesitant. Make an effort to learn as much as possible about the subject by doing some research, enrolling in classes, and feigning courage while doing so.

CHAPTER NINE

Treatment Options for Phobias

Treatment options for Phobias that do not Involve Medication. For example, persons who suffer from phobias such as agoraphobia (an uncontrolled dread of open spaces), claustrophobia (anxiety about being in small areas), or panic attacks (anxiety about being alone) may have phobias such as flying, heights, insects, or even attending to school (fear of going outside, of being away from the security of the home, or of being alone).

It is believed that 10% of the population has at least one phobia, although most individuals are able to keep it under control by avoiding the stimuli or concealing their anxieties. Phobias are only considered significant when the fear becomes crippling and affects daily life to the point that it needs to be adjusted or avoided in everyday settings. Fear might be caused by an unidentified factor, or it can be the outcome of an event that has been with you for a long time. In certain cases, it might be caused by an organic ailment, such as epilepsy or brain damage, or it can be passed along from one generation to the next by parents, teachers, and other caregivers. People with borderline diabetes or sugar sensitivity are more likely to experience panic and anxiety as a consequence of low blood sugar. Stress, worry, and panic may all lead to phobias as well. Anxious, nervy, or easily agitated persons are more susceptible to phobias than those who are calmer. People with phobias display symptoms such as extreme anxiety when presented with their fearful subject. Breathlessness, palpitations and sweating are among the most common physical symptoms.

To avoid a confrontation with the object of their apprehension, a victim may go to great lengths. Learning to Manage Patients may be able to assist themselves, at least in certain cases, by gradually increasing their exposure levels. People who suffer from a severe fear are unable to even contemplate it. Drawing images of the object of fear, looking at photos in a magazine, and so on, are all ways to begin the process of conquering a phobia. If you're afraid of flying because of a situational phobia, your doctor may advise you to visit an airport and watch aircraft take off and land. It is possible to go as far as the departure lounge on your next visit (many airlines offer sessions for phobics and do not consider this unusual).

A third visit may include a ride in an aircraft, or at least an electronic flying simulator. You will eventually learn to overcome your apprehensiveness. Step by step, that's what I say. Make to-do lists and maintain a journal to track your progress. Even if you feel like you're taking two steps back for every one stride forward, a journal may help you keep track of the progress you've made and how you've come to accept your current circumstance. Overcoming a phobia requires learning to control the terror, which may be accomplished with enough effort. Panic might be debilitating and seem insurmountable at first, but with practice and distance from the symptoms, you can learn to shut them out.

To overcome a phobia, it may take a number of panic attacks, but gradually it becomes evident that panic attacks are a thing of the past and can be overcome. Treatment Relaxation and desensitisation strategies may be used as part of psychotherapy treatment. Borax and sulphur are good for fear of heights, whereas Lycopodium, Gelsemium, and Anarcardium are good for stage fright when performing in front of an audience.

CHAPTER TEN

A fear of being rejected is the root of procrastination

Have you ever been paralysed by the dread of rejection when it comes to marketing? Reaching out to other people, fear of failing or fear of doing something wrong? Many of us, I believe, are born with it. As a result, we're unable to go out and recruit new customers. It's time to put an end to it. In this post, you'll learn precisely how I overcame a few of my personal anxieties and got out there in a major manner.

Has procrastination ever slowed you down in your marketing efforts and you couldn't figure out where it was coming from? Several of my private customers have experienced this in the recent past, and each time, we discovered that the true culprit was anxiety rather than procrastination.

Maybe it's happened to you as well? There are several fears associated with reaching out to others. These include fear of rejection, fear of failing, fear of succeeding, and worry of doing something incorrectly. I don't believe I know anybody who hasn't had some kind of dread of rejection when it comes to self-promotion.. For many of us,

I believe, it comes naturally. It's a problem since it prevents us from attracting new customers. And everything has to come to an end.

Avoiding the sale, reaching out, asking for assistance, giving a speech in front of a crowd, requesting recommendations, and partnering with strategic partnerships are all hindered by a fear of rejection. Your lack of marketing will result in your lack of customers in six months, I have said this many times before.

So, now that you know that you're unable to go forward because of fear, what do you do? My customers and I have done a lot of study on this over the years. I've devoured books, special reports, and whatever else that could be found on the topic. There's a problem, though, since most people gloss over what you should do.

There is a lot of discussions about altering your perspective, focusing on the positive, and so on. That's OK, but I'm not certain it's a viable solution. The concerns and limiting ideas that have previously hindered me, as well as those that I observe in my clients, compelled me to learn how to overcome them.

Client Attraction isn't the only game in town when it comes to finding new customers (marketing). If you don't deal with the inner aspect of Client Attraction (your attitude and beliefs), you'll continue to do the same things (and make the same money) for years to come.. To be honest, I'd rather continue to develop and produce more.

In order to discover the solution, I conducted an introspective inquiry of my own. The actions I've taken to improve my own personal growth and development, which I'm still working on, have helped me dispel the limiting ideas and concerns that prevent us from promoting (and shining, personally) to our full potential.

What should you do?

Identify the core fear or limiting thought that's keeping you from pursuing marketing. You're afraid you'll make a mistake, you're afraid to ask for what you want, you're afraid to say no to someone because you're afraid of being rejected. For the purpose of argument, let's take the fear of rejection, as it's a major concern for my clients.

Think back to when you were a kid. The first time you were rejected was when you were a child. It's a good idea to jot it down. Write down whatever you see in this assignment. I'm not kidding. To obtain results, do this.) If you feel stuck, go back to the first thing that came to mind as you read the assignment. Even if you don't think so, that's generally the most important one to take care of initially.

1. Make a list of all the times in your life when you felt rejected (by your parents, kids in grade school, high school, the dating years, cheerleading or sports tryouts, the working world, and, of course, since being self-employed).

4. Now consider the meaning you ascribed to each of those occurrences. There are a lot of people who believe they aren't talented enough, stupid enough, or unlucky enough to earn a lot of money. This is where the mend starts, so take your time with it. Consider yourself a tough grader.

5. Make a separate list of how these MEANINGS you've made have stifled your progress in life. Have you stopped contacting me? Have you ceased to take chances? Did you bury yourself somewhere? Did you

miss out on chances that may have made you a better person? Make a list of all of them.

Return to your list of meanings and question, "What if what I THINK occurred wasn't truly the case?" 6. What I mean is this: While "I'm ugly," "I'm not likeable," and "I don't like this person" are common reasons for being rejected by high school crushes, consider alternative possibilities. Could they have been seeing someone else in the back of their minds? Could it be that they were afraid to speak up? Is it possible that they were attracted to someone of the opposite sex? Write it all down.

7. There are many more reasons why they wouldn't have done the "correct" thing for you, and this is only a sampling of them. This is a list of things you should look at, and I can promise that what you think occurred is not what happened. If someone did anything wrong, we'll never know the reason for it since everyone's writing is on the wall (we might never know what was going on for them at that time).

8. Reassess the limiting thought or fear that's holding you back. What if you were really rejected? It's possible that anything else may have caused this. Does it really matter that you've been impacted by this for the rest of your life and that you've missed out on chances because of what one person said or did? The question is whether or not the event is actually worth a halt in your marketing efforts.

Choose an ALTERNATE explanation for what occurred and let go of your worry.

9. You have earned the right to no longer be stymied in your tracks. The things that people said or did to you in the past weren't fair, and it's time to let them go. I want you to succeed, and I know that you deserve it.

If you can't shake the fear, simply feel it and do what you need to do nonetheless. "Successful individuals feel the dread, too, and they do what it takes nonetheless," is a well-known quote. That's what I've observed. When I find myself getting stuck, I apply the method outlined above and then simply push through until I finish what I'm working on. Strangely, it never comes close to being as horrible as I had imagined it would be. The best part is that every time you overcome a fear, you strengthen that muscle. Limiting fears and beliefs lose their power over time.

Don't forget about the workout above. Spend an afternoon or an hour figuring out what's holding you back. To begin with, it may seem daunting, but I tell you that it becomes second nature once you put yourself out there and do it. In the end, it's a liberating experience.

You'll start doing more, taking advantage of chances, and achieving greater outcomes in marketing as a consequence of this training. Profitability and the ability to live the life you choose are directly related when you have more paying customers and produce more outcomes. The view from the other side of fear is SUCCESS, according to what I once read. Do you have what it takes?

It's time to change things up if you've overcome your worries and are still unsure how to attract customers in a manner that feels effortless and real to you.

CHAPTER ELEVEN

strategies for overcoming fear

Here are some strategies to calm your fears.> > When we're afraid, we're less likely to take risks and enjoy life more. In our minds, fear tells us, "You'll never succeed, so why even try?". Frightens us into silence.

Fear-reduction tips: some ideas.

It's common for fear to get in the way of us living happier, more rewarding lives. In our minds, fear tells us, "You'll never succeed, so why even try?" There are voices in our heads that tell us we're not good enough, and we succumb to their temptations.

When we let fear govern our lives, we lose out on chances and discard individuals and events that may help us achieve our objectives. Procrastination, for example, is a sort of fear that manifests itself in a variety of ways. Here are some techniques to minimise and overcome fear.

The first step is to write down all of your anxieties and how they impact your life.

Fear of not being good enough or of making changes, in general, maybe the reason for delaying taking action on some topics. Your time on this planet is finite. There's a reason they're called deadlines!

Pay attention to your inner dialogue. There are many of us who make pronouncements such as, "I'll never be able to obtain that job," rather than actual conversations with myself. This is a death sentence for your brain since there is nothing for it to work on. It's on an extended vacation now!

Begin by posing questions to yourself. For example, you can ask yourself, "How can I make making this speech fun?" You've given your mind something to do now! You shouldn't anticipate a solution immediately away, but you should be on the lookout for changes and circumstances that reveal hints.

Asking yourself questions instead of making sweeping (negative) comments should become a habit.

Learn from your errors by redefining what constitutes a "mistake". Don't beat yourself up over previous failures, and don't be afraid to start new relationships, employment, or anything else for that matter. That's a waste of time. Learn from your mistakes by referring to them as "opportunities for growth".

Stay away from folks who are negative and "fearful" in their outlook on life and seek out those who are helpful.

Study the concepts and attributes that underlie successful people's actions, as well as their way of thinking and attitude. Seek role models in your own neighbourhood that embody the ideals you want to achieve. Take a page from their book.

If you like someone's qualities, know that you have the same potential to develop them in yourself. What other way would you be able to tell it apart? Make a list of the characteristics you admire in others, and then consider how you can recognise and cultivate those same characteristics in yourself.

No one's history has to dictate their present. Recognize and be ready to let go of your history. No matter how many times you wake up, there will always be something new you can do or consider.

The best way to stay on track is to write down your objectives and the steps you need to take every day. The more progress you make toward your objectives, the more confident you will feel about yourself and the less fearful you will be.

In addition to that, Hire a Personal Trainer! Alternatively, you might have a friend or family member to help you overcome your apprehension and reach your objectives.

The following is a list of all of the characters in the original text: A Personal and Business Coach, Julie Plenty specialises in helping individuals improve their self-esteem via coaching programmes. She is of the opinion that an excessive number of individuals do not live up to their full potential. Self-esteem issues cause many people to fall short of their full potential and live lives that are far from happy.

CHAPTER TWELVE

How to deal with the fear of being alone

In many cases, the dread of success is the culmination of earlier phobias. The worry may stem from a concern about disappointing someone, such as a coach, father, or teacher, who has placed their trust in you. On the other hand, the dread of success, on the other hand, is not a fear that can be generalised since success might mean various things to different people.

Do you ever worry that you'll be alone for the rest of your life? You can't go a day without seeing at least one person attempting to find a partner, or forgetting someone, or dealing with someone. One of the most basic human desires is the need to be loved and to be loved in return. In addition, when someone is terrified of being single, he or she may have the debilitating belief that he or she will always be alone or that he or she is flawed in some way. There is, however, nothing to be afraid of. Your value and worthiness need to be recognised and appreciated. The dread of being alone should not dictate your actions.

Begin by being kind to yourself. Every aspect of our lives is scrutinised by an inner voice. Self-talk has a significant influence on our emotions since we participate in both good and negative self-talk. This leads to a rise in feelings of self-worthlessness when your inner voice tells you that you're incompetent, unattractive, a failure, and so on. Do not be too hard on yourself. In the end, it doesn't matter what other people think of you since you know the truth. You must forgive yourself for your past errors and order your inner voice to shut up. You'll convince yourself that no one wants to be with you if you keep dwelling on your flaws.

The more confident you are, the more valuable you become. It's enticing to have self-assurance because when you value yourself, others do, too. Now is the time to work on building your self-esteem and confidence. The more confident and self-loving you seem, the more at ease you will be with yourself. Start learning as much as you can about the topic and putting what you've learned into practice as soon as possible. Find out how much fun you can have with yourself by trying new things and experimenting. Positive self-affirmations and mindfulness meditation may help you overcome the stress and negativity in your life.

When it comes to the opposite sex, change your mind. You may have had a bad experience with someone that caused you to change your mind about the opposite sex. You may think that all guys are jerks or that all women are money diggers. However, this is not true. Many fine men and women are out there yearnings for real love, though. As a result, your anxiety about being alone will grow since you're continuously convincing yourself that there is no one decent out there for you.

In particular, women, in particular, are under a lot of pressure in today's culture to be in a relationship. No matter how successful you are, you are compelled to feel that if you don't have someone in your life, you will never be happy. Being single is seen as a failure as a result of this. However, the reality is that you are not a failure at all. You might be dating someone right now if you wanted to, but you may want to wait or need some space to recover from a prior relationship.

Reframe your perspective on being a single person. If you change your outlook on yourself, you will no longer be afraid of being single. As a single person, you have the chance to develop and find yourself.

CHAPTER THIRTEEN

No need to be concerned

What frightens us? What does it mean to be afraid? We don't know what to do about it. We all experience fear at some point in our lives, and to varying degrees. I performed some research of my own and discovered that fear of public speaking and fear of achievement were among the most common fears.

Earlier this month, I got an email that asked me to take a survey on what I dreaded the most. To avoid getting any more unwanted emails at the time, I decided not to respond to the email. However, I began to contemplate the concept of terror itself. What frightens us? What does it mean to be afraid? We don't know what to do about it. We all experience fear at some point in our lives, and to varying degrees. I performed some research of my own and discovered that fear of public speaking and fear of achievement were among the most common fears.

Public speaking phobia

According to the findings of a recent study, the fear of public speaking appears to be more common than death. When it comes to public speaking, most individuals don't realise they have a fear of public speaking because they don't know why. However, psychological studies have shown that virtually everyone who suffers from public speaking anxiety suffered some type of trauma as a child, be it big or small.

Success Anxiety

Fear of success is a well-known and widespread phobia. To be considered a success, one must be able to say that they have achieved their aim. Success may be defined in a variety of ways, including money, celebrity, or power. Achieving one's goals is a rewarding experience. How come so many of us are terrified of success, whether we realise it or not? It all boils down to how we define and measure success.

When we eventually achieve our objectives, we are more concerned with the bad elements than the positive ones. In our minds, we may recall a person who was mocked for having "too much money" because of their success. Perhaps we've heard that it's easier for the impoverished to get into paradise or that successful people believe they're superior to others. As a result, when we achieve success, we get anxious about what others will say and think about us. In many cases, we thwart our progress.

We have no qualms about succeeding, even though we are terrified of it. Because we fear the consequences of success, we avoid it at all costs. "The good life" conjures up feelings of shame in us. We're afraid that if we make our pals envious, they won't like us anymore. We're worried about having to put in more effort now that we've been elevated. We're worried about having to pay a lot of money in taxes. Somebody may attempt to take us from here. Now and then, we ponder what would happen if we suddenly found ourselves without any money.

One of the strongest emotions

Fear is an emotion, and it manifests itself in a variety of ways in each of us. There are several ways to tell whether you're afraid, such as a short breath, sweaty hands, and an upset stomach. You may also have a headache or an inability to talk or think effectively. People have been known to end their own lives as a result of their fear. Fear is at the root of all of today's "isms," including racism, chauvinism, classism, and sexism. Fear is a powerful motivator for conflict and criminal activity.

Fear robs us of our imagination, creativity, freedom, and tranquilly. To pursue our aspirations, we must overcome fear. Fear may ruin relationships and even make us sick. F E A R is a four-letter acronym for the most potent kind of negative emotion.

Think about it: we're all so miserable and miserable because of something that doesn't exist at all except for the meaning or perspective that we assign to it. The only reason our anxieties persist is that we individually infuse them with a life of our own. We are the ones who keep our anxieties alive by nurturing, feeding, and acknowledging them.

Stories and Imaginations of the Past

What we fear is dependent on our particular perceptions, which in turn are based on tales we've heard and imaginations we've created.

Is there any other way to explain the reality that we all experience terror in various ways? Many individuals, for example, have a soft spot for dogs. However, some individuals are afraid of dogs. Some people keep snakes as pets because they like their venomous nature. Snakes terrify some people to the point of physical harm, while others are terrified of them to the point of physical paralysis.

In many cases, we have no idea what stories are underlying our fears. Several of us suffer from anxiety attacks and terror because of a statement another youngster made to us as a child. That is to say, we are allowing a kid from our past to dictate our present-day behaviour and health.

Let Go of Your Anxiety

If we want to overcome our anxiety, we must alter our preconceptions about a person, event, or thing. Let it be a person, an event, or something else entirely. The dread of things that have not occurred and may never occur is a common one for many people. Because we are afraid of what the future holds, we are unable to appreciate our life now. We have the power to free ourselves from the shackles of our memories and fantasies.

Emotional Freedom Techniques (EFT), Neuro-Linguistic Programming (NLP), or hypnosis may help if you're paralysed by dread of anything. If you're interested in learning more about these strategies, I urge you to do so. There are a variety of approaches that each of them uses to de-traumatize the past while also identifying and resolving the underlying beliefs that prevent us from achieving our goals.

In my experience, these kinds of techniques may instantly alleviate anxiety. Instead of only treating the symptoms, these treatments and other comparable processes attack the root cause of the anxiety.

A Call to Action

Fear, on the other hand, is a good thing since it serves as a signal for change. We would hope that things would change for the better if someone pointed a gun at us. If we're lucky, we'll come up with a solution without being hurt. Fear of harming a kid has compelled parents to develop physical and mental fortitude they never imagined possible.

It's the same with our daily anxieties. Let dread serve as a compass that points you in the right direction. Get out of your way. If someone, something, or somewhere is making us anxious, it's possible that we need information. The most essential thing to remember is to make progress toward loving someone. Self-acceptance begins with self-acceptance. Everyone and everything should be cherished and adored. The strongest feeling is love. True love is the antidote to fear.

We Have the Ability to Overcome Any Form of Fear We Face.

Fear stems mostly, in my view, from a misunderstanding of our place in God's and the universe's grand scheme. The absence of faith breeds fear. Doubt and dread arise when we don't have faith in who we are and what we're capable of.

The tragedy is inevitable. There is no guarantee that things will always go according to your plans. There will inevitably be those who are eager to point out your flaws. Rather than deal with their issues, these folks will rather point out your inadequacies. Do not hand over your authority to them.

None of us can be described as your average Joe. All of us are awe-inspiring gods and goddesses. Everyone has unstoppable power if they just recognise and accept it. I have to remind myself of this from time to time. This is what I have to say: "Fear, you've got to leave. You have no influence at all in this situation. " Free web content is like turning on a light switch and seeing what it truly is: nothing.

CHAPTER FOURTEEN

How to Overcome Your Phobia

Fear of rejection, failure, success, humiliation, criticism, and uncertainty are just a few of the concerns that hold us back in business.

Fear of rejection, failure, success, humiliation, criticism, and uncertainty are just a few of the concerns that hold us back in business.

For you to be successful, you must develop a lifelong habit of doing the things you are afraid of.

The list goes on and on. Because I've worked with hundreds of entrepreneurs, you surely know that I've seen how people limit themselves in their businesses and personal lives by giving in to fear and self-doubt. The problem is, they don't even know it. This is what I'm saying... To acquire what they want—a change—people will say they'll do just about anything.

Self-doubt and fear of failure are common obstacles that prevent entrepreneurs from reaching their full potential in their businesses and personal lives.

It's a very different scenario when the rubber strikes the road. As a general rule, many people are unwilling to take the necessary actions or put in the effort required to achieve their goals. It's the constant uncertainty and worry that keeps them rethinking every decision they make to develop their company and generate more money.

It's time to get started on your client attraction project. Take some time to reflect on the following issues: What are you prepared to give up for long-term gain? If so, are you prepared to go to any lengths to accomplish your goals? Are you willing to speak with whoever has to be spoken to? Is it possible for you to accomplish something you've never done? Is it possible for you to go beyond what you're used to doing?

Bibliography

Making Friends With Fear. (2022). Articlesfactory.com. http://www.articlesfactory.com/articles/self-help/making-friends-with-fear.html

Feel the Fear and Do It Anyway. (2022). Articlesfactory.com. http://www.articlesfactory.com/articles/business/feel-the-fear-and-do-it-anyway.html

Quanta's Jim Britt - Letting Go of FEAR. (2022). Articlesfactory.com. http://www.articlesfactory.com/articles/self-help/quantas-jim-britt-letting-go-of-fear.html

Cultivate A Friendship With Death. (2022). Articlesfactory.com. http://www.articlesfactory.com/articles/self-help/cultivate-a-friendship-with-death.html

Law Of Attraction - Why Fear is The One Secret Holding You Back. (2022). Articlesfactory.com. http://www.articlesfactory.com/articles/social-issues/law-of-attraction-why-fear-is-the-one-secret-holding-you-back.html

Do You Live in Fear? (2022). Articlesfactory.com. http://www.articlesfactory.com/articles/ecommerce/do-you-live-in-fear.html

Starting a New Business. (2022). Articlesfactory.com. http://www.articlesfactory.com/articles/business/starting-a-new-business.html

Changing Fear into Excitement. (2022). Articlesfactory.com. http://www.articlesfactory.com/articles/motivational/changing-fear-into-excitement.html

Alternative Treatment For Phobias. (2022). Articlesfactory.com. http://www.articlesfactory.com/articles/health/alternative-treatment-for-phobias.html

It's Not Procrastination, It's Fear of Rejection (Get Past It and Get Marketing). (2022). Articlesfactory.com. http://www.articlesfactory.com/articles/business/its-not-procrastination-its-fear-of-rejection-get-past-it-and-get-marketing.html

Comfort. The Internal Dental Marketing That Patients Will Truly Appreciate... (2022). Articlesfactory.com. http://www.articlesfactory.com/articles/marketing/comfort-the-internal-dental-marketing-that-patients-will-truly-appreciate.html

10 ways to deal with fear. (2022). Articlesfactory.com. http://www.articlesfactory.com/articles/health/10-ways-to-deal-with-fear.html

Fear of being single and how to overcome it. (2022). Articlesfactory.com. http://www.articlesfactory.com/articles/motivational/fear-of-being-single-and-how-to-overcome-it.html

Fear Be Gone. (2022). Articlesfactory.com. http://www.articlesfactory.com/articles/self-help/fear-be-gone.html

How to Break Through Fear. (2022). Articlesfactory.com. http://www.articlesfactory.com/articles/marketing/how-to-break-through-fear.html

Fear | Copyright Free Content. (2018). Copyrightfreecontent.com. https://www.copyrightfreecontent.com/?s=Fear

9 798885 556804

Printed by Libri Plureos GmbH in Hamburg, Germany